L 8.2

On C-

The Revd Dr Hora...
Chairman of the Con... ...on Texts
and the English Langu... ...i Consultation
and is Professor of W... ...p and Preaching at
Boston University School of Theology.

The Revd Joseph Russell is a priest of the Episcopal
Church in Cleveland, Ohio, and is the present chair
of the Consultation on Common Texts, on which he
represents the Episcopal Church.

On Common Ground

The story of the
Revised Common Lectionary

Horace T. Allen, Jr
& Joseph P. Russell

CANTERBURY
PRESS
Norwich

© The Consultation on Common Texts (CCT) 1998

First published in 1998 by The Canterbury Press Norwich (a
publishing imprint of Hymns Ancient & Modern Limited, a
registered charity)
St Mary's Works, St Mary's Plain,
Norwich, Norfolk, NR3 3BH

British Library Cataloguing in Publication Data

A catalogue record for this book is available from the British
Library

ISBN 1-85311-219-4

Typeset by David Gregson Associates, Beccles, Suffolk
and printed in Great Britain by Biddles Ltd,
Guildford and Kings Lynn

Contents

Contents

Introduction

Sola scriptura, sola gratia, sola fidei!

These three pithy slogans became the battle cry of the Protestant Reformations of the sixteenth and succeeding centuries. As in all polemic situations, the positions taken and assumptions made were probably too sharp and antithetical for imitation by subsequent moments of history. And their use here, at the outset of the recounting of a significant and impressive ecumenical development, is certainly not meant, in any way, to reopen old wounds in the still-divided Body of Christ on earth.

The first of these phrases, however, is much of the inspiration of the enterprise recounted by this volume. What does it mean? Most basically it affirms the primacy of the canon of Holy Scripture as the locus of the definitive and authoritative message of salvation in Jesus Christ. In its polemic context it was meant to guard against what the Reformers took to be encroachments in this regard by the Church's *magisterium* by which tradition not only amplified or explicated that message but even further, also defined it, especially in the direction of 'nature' and human works. This theo-

logical altercation can be heard as recently as in documents of the Second Vatican Council such as *De
Revelatione*.[1]

When one remembers that the Church's liturgy is a
principal means of the 'traditioning process', and also
that the Holy Scriptures have always been a primary
shaper of both the form and the content of these
liturgies, one realizes how critical it is that the liturgical use of Scripture reflects the richest content of *sola
scriptura*. As this writer has contended in another place,

> To read the Bible at worship is to read the Bible in a new
> way, in community. It is to read the Bible as prayer, praise,
> and proclamation. That is probably why, in [the] Scottish
> tradition, the beginning of worship was signaled by the
> carrying into the assembly of the massive pulpit Bible by
> the 'beadle'.[2]

This liturgical use of the Scripture was certainly the
driving force behind a number of the liturgical reforms
of the various Protestant reform movements. One
thinks first of the impulse for the use of the vernacular,
and in particular for the biblical texts to be clearly
proclaimed (for which the advent of moveable type
printing was a providential means). And, as Barth has
trenchantly observed, proclamation actually includes all
those other liturgical texts such as hymns, prayers,
acclamations and sacramental rites:

> ... primarily and decisively, preaching and the sacraments;
> with regard to the latter, which, as *verba visibilia* in

actions, belong to a special order, the main thing will likewise be the oral proclamation accompanying them, the 'doctrine' of the sacraments which is significant for the meaning of their administration in vogue at the time- ...Further, prayers and singings in Church cannot be treated as absolutely without dogmatic importance. Liturgy and hymn-books also claim to be taken seriously, on the score that their contents consist of human words, and that they too may be effective as proclamation...[3]

In that connection one must bear in mind also the several great explosions of psalmody in the sixteenth century, biblical paraphrases in the seventeenth century and hymnody from the eighteenth century to the present day, as compelling evidence of a recovery of Scripture as the fount and inspiration of the people's praise.

Another quite obvious recovery was that of preaching as a liturgical event. Daring as it may have seemed at the time, it was quite essential that *sola scriptura* be played out into a methodical and ministerial event – as part of the liturgy – wherein (in Barth's astonishing phrase) the preacher 'will add to what has been read from the Bible something from his own head and heart'.[4] In certain parts of the Reformation tradition, that homiletical method was tied directly to the succession of chapters of the biblical books so as in effect to recover the synagogal and primitive ecclesial custom of continuous reading (*lectio continua*). Such a practice can be identified in such historically distant documents as Justin Martyr's *Apology* (*c*. AD 155) and the *Westminster Directory for Worship* (AD 1645).

Although one must admit that this process could produce a kind of didacticism which ill fits the liturgy, it was with a sure instinct that reformed churches also provided extensive institutions for catechetical instruction as is evidenced by certain of the classic sixteenth-century catechisms such as Heidelberg (1563) with its Lord's Day dating (through the year) of the 129 questions and answers.

In all these ways, and others, the attempt was to ensure that Church tradition would maintain its responsibility and accountability to the principle of *sola scriptura*. The *Revised Common Lectionary* may thus be seen in this context as a continuing affirmation of that preoccupation and, in our own time, the happy product of a non-polemical, thoroughly ecumenical process which is indeed, the story of the *Revised Common Lectionary*.

That story, because it does involve the Scriptures, and is profoundly ecumenical, needs to be placed in the succession of several post-Reformation developments in the Western Churches (i.e. Roman Catholic, Anglican and Protestant). These developments might be defined as (1) the nineteenth-century historico-critical biblical studies movement; (2) the nineteenth- and twentieth-century liturgical movement; (3) the twentieth-century response of neo-orthodoxy; and (4) the more recent ecumenical movement from the late 1940s through the formation of the World Council of Churches and

Introduction

its notable Faith and Order paper No.III, *Baptism, Eucharist and Ministry.*

(1) The Historico-Critical Movement in Biblical Studies.

This movement of the late nineteenth century has transformed the Church's understanding of its canon. The application of scientific methods to the analysis of literary genres and forms opened up the fields of exegesis, interpretation and hermeneutics. Although at first this was a Protestant (and largely German) phenomenon it gradually influenced most of Western Protestantism and eventually Roman Catholic scholarship as well. (One notes the important 'Document on the Interpretation of the Bible in the Church' published by the Holy See on April 23, 1993). This phenomenon, however, created violent controversy in the United States, where the situation was characterized by a near-total stand-off between literalist and liberal assumptions (as Leander Keck so perceptively puts it, the former 'over-canonized' and the latter 'under-canonized' the sacred texts). The effect in the twentieth century was to free the Churches to use the Scriptures in ways which respected their own inner orderings and which took note of the process whereby they were themselves, in their formation and early editing, the work and reflection of the Early Churches. Thus to uncover the reciprocal relationship between text and ecclesial context was to anticipate and enable later schools such as canon criticism and, of course, the lectionary-building of the mid-to-late twentieth century, on Catholic and non-Catholic sides alike.

(2) The Nineteenth- and Twentieth-Century Liturgical Movement.

Several traditions in the late nineteenth century began to uncover early patterns of worship from the patristic age onwards. Pre-eminent in this field was the Roman Catholic Church, particularly under the influence of the Benedictines who had always celebrated the Daily Office, the *opus Dei*, with particular care and discipline. The Roman efforts were paralleled in Anglicanism by the Tractarians and also in both Lutheran and Reformed circles. The mid nineteenth-century Mercersburg Movement in the German Reformed Church of the USA, spearheaded by Philip Schaff and John Williamson Nevin, created great interest and was probably greatly influenced by the (European) Catholic Apostolic Church. In Scotland, the Church Service Society was founded in 1865, begetting an American equivalent almost one century later. The initial thrust of these movements tended to be archaeological (*ad fontes*) and they were often criticized as being 'romantic'. Our own time, however, has seen the fruits of these efforts, and nowhere more so than in the Roman Catholic Church with its first-fruits of Vatican II, *Sacrosanctam Concilium* (1963). This led directly to the achievement referred to in this volume as the *Revised Common Lectionary*.

(3) The Twentieth-Century Response of Neo-orthodoxy.

This development is termed a 'response' because of its relationship to the biblical studies movement. It too was largely German (and Swiss) in its origins. There, by the beginning of the twentieth century, one might have been able to draw a road-map of theology showing three regions: (i) Classic Roman Catholic/Thomist, (ii) Protestant scholasticism (Lutheran and Reformed) and (iii) Protestant liberalism. The revolution created in biblical studies opened up a completely new relationship between the Scriptures and these theological traditions. The figure of Karl Barth was central to this as he essayed anew a kind of Reformation biblical method for doing theology. It is not without interest that he began this as a local pastor, overwhelmed by the liturgical task of preaching, and that his first major publication was a commentary on the Letter to the Romans (1921), not unlike Luther's own beginnings as a Reformer. Because of his interest in the Scriptures and in Reformation and Patristic theology, this development too was encouraging of liturgical reform and of a reconsideration of the place of the Scriptures in public worship.

(4) The Ecumenical Movement

This most well-known and organized impulse has been

essential to the lectionary 'story' recounted here. It made possible a broadly-based convergence of all the strands of scholarship listed above and the kind of inter-penetration which could inevitably only result in a vast re-ordering of the *lex orandi* of many churches. It is surely no accident that possibly the most impressive document ever published by the World Council of Churches is its theological and liturgical *Baptism, Eucharist and Ministry*, especially as it is the first conciliar document to be submitted by the parent body to its member bodies for official reception. Its witness to a widely shared liturgical convergence is every bit as impressive as the particular instance of such ecumenism as the reception by so many churches of the Roman-Ecumenical three-year lectionary systems of the *Ordo lectionum Missae* (1969) and its derivative, the *Revised Common Lectionary* (1992).

This brings us to a detailed chronicle of the ways in which the *Ordo lectionum Missae* of 1969 inspired by Vatican II has given birth to an ecumenically developed and accepted lectionary table.

Part One

CHAPTER 1

The Story of the *Revised Common Lectionary:* 1969–1999

Our story begins with a declaration made in the above-mentioned Second Vatican Council's 'Constitution on the Sacred Liturgy':

The treasures of the Bible are to be opened up more lavishly, so that a richer share in God's word may be provided for the faithful. In this way a more representative portion of Holy Scripture will be read to the people in the course of a prescribed number of years.[5]

This 'prescribed number of years' turned out to be three, to make possible the 'course' or continuous reading of each of the three Synoptic gospels in turn: Matthew – Year A; Mark – Year B; and Luke – Year C. A working group was set up following the Council (*Coetus XI*) to carry out this conciliar

3

mandate. Its Secretary, Fr Gaston Fontaine CRIC, identified the liturgical focus of this work as follows:

> The proclamation of Scripture within the context of the community gathered for worship is itself an assurance of Christ's presence. The liturgy of the word and the liturgy of the eucharist, 'so closely connected with each other that they form but one single act of worship', makes us sharers in the faith of Christ crucified and risen and, through him who is the crown of it all, causes us to enter more fully into the whole historic work of salvation.[6]

Coetus XI set about its work in obedience to the Council and, at the urging of one of its members, Fr Godfrey Diekmann OSB, took serious note of the 'ecumenical ramifications of lectionary preparation'.[7] By 1969 it had produced a new table of readings for the Roman Catholic Church: *Ordo lectionum Missae*.[8] This table proposed three readings for each Lord's Day over a three-year cycle. In addition, a psalm was provided for use following the Old Testament pericope. This table is now in universal use in that Church. A supplemental second edition was published in 1981[9] which in no way altered the 1969 pattern but simply added to it and more amply rehearsed its rationale. This 1969 table was almost instantly taken up by a number of other Churches, as described by this writer in his 'Introduction' to the 1983 publication of the *Common Lectionary*:

The wisdom embodied in the work of *Coetus XI*, now in universal use in the churches that follow the Roman rite, has been attested by a completely unexpected and salutary development, particularly in North America, but also in other parts of the world. That is the appropriation of the Roman Lectionary by more than a few Protestant and Anglican churches. This process began with the publication in 1970 of an edition thereof in *The Worshipbook*, a service book jointly produced by three Presbyterian churches in the United States. Shortly thereafter the Episcopal and Lutheran churches included it in preliminary studies which resulted in its inclusion in the Episcopal *Draft Proposed Book of Common Prayer*, and also the *Lutheran Book of Worship*. In the meantime the United Methodist Church in the USA made an edition available in 1976 and the Disciples of Christ as well as the United Church of Christ adopted for voluntary use the Presbyterian version. These developments were materially assisted by the publication of a consensus edition in pamphlet form by the ecumenical Consultation on Church Union, representing (at that time) nine Protestant denominations seeking fuller unity. In Canada the United

5

Church has undertaken experimental use of the three-year lectionary in a number of parishes, and the Anglican Church has published a pamphlet (1980) making it available.[10]

This proliferation in the 1970s of edited versions of the original Roman table was ecumenically encouraging but also dismaying. No less than five or six subtly varied forms of the Roman table came into circulation in North America, in each of which the method of calculation of which lessons to use on the Sundays after Pentecost, for instance, differed. Attempts by local clergy to meet together for sermon planning were plagued by this diversity, and published materials for homiletical work were confronted by multiple options. Increasingly the cry went up for some standardization.

An ecumenical body which had been in existence since 1964 – the Consultation on Common Texts (CCT)[11] – took the lead by convening a meeting of representatives of some thirteen churches from Canada and the United States, in Washington, DC, on 29–31 March, 1978. There was registered general agreement on the excellence of the Roman table and the desirability of greater uniformity in its use. Minutes of the meeting record that a consensus table of readings should be drawn up for recommendation to the Churches and that in particular there was need to revise the Old Testament selections, at least for the Sundays in Ordinary Time after Pentecost:

> ...in order to provide readings that are more completely representative of the Hebrew Bible and not simply prophetic or typological; this includes the possibility of aligning the Old Testament passage with the New Testament selection rather than with the Gospel.[12]

As a result of this action, the Consultation, chaired at that time by this writer, set up a working group, the North American Committee on Calendar and Lectionary (NACCL), presided over by the Revd Dr Lewis A. Briner, a minister of the United Presbyterian Church who had been instrumental in the inclusion of the Roman *Ordo* in that church's *Worshipbook*. Membership of the Committee at one time or another included pastors and scholars from the Roman Catholic, Episcopal, Presbyterian, Lutheran and United Methodist Churches. The Committee met twice yearly and generally worked by delegating selected portions of the lectionary to designated members. Its working principles were described by this writer to the 1981 meeting of *Societas Liturgica* in Paris as follows:

> 1. The basic calendar and structure of three readings presupposed by the Roman Lectionary are assumed.

2. The Gospel pericopes are assumed with only minor textual rearrangement to accommodate churches which use a Bible for liturgical use rather than a Lectionary.

3. The New Testament pericopes are largely accepted with some lengthening of pericopes and minor textual re-arrangement to include contextual material such as apostolic and personal greetings and local ecclesial issues.

4. The typological choice of Old Testament pericopes has been addressed in that this has been the area of most serious criticism of the lectionary from Catholic and Protestant scholars and pastors. In response, the Committee has proposed a revision of the Roman table for a number of Sundays of the Year in each of the three cycles. The lessons are still typologically controlled by the Gospel, but in a broader way than Sunday by Sunday, in order to make possible semi-continuous reading of some significant Old Testament narratives.[13]

The finished work of this committee was published in 1983 as the Consultation's proposal. It then went through a testing period of three complete cycles (nine years in all). Towards the end of this time, the Consultation set up a Lectionary Task Force which, after several years of soliciting evaluations, published the *Revised Common Lectionary* in 1992.[14]

8

This undertaking in North America created considerable interest in other parts of the English-speaking world, especially since churches in Great Britain, working together through the Joint Liturgical Group, had published a two-year lectionary and calendar in 1967, which immediately came into widespread use. This interest coincided with a sensed need by the North American Consultation and the Joint Liturgical Group in Britain to take another look at the common liturgical texts which had been produced and published by the earlier International Consultation on English Texts as *Prayers We Have in Common*.[15] That body had met last in London in 1974. The result was a consultation at the time of the 1983 *Societas Liturgica* Congress in Vienna. It was decided to form a new international body with a broader agenda than that of the International Consultation in order to address not only the matter of common texts, but also the matter of lectionaries. This body met first in Boston, Massachusetts as the English Language Liturgical Consultation (ELLC) in August 1985. Representatives were present from the North American Consultation, the British Joint Liturgical Group, the Roman Catholic International Commission on English in the Liturgy, the Australian Consultation on Liturgy and the Liturgical Committee of the South African Church Unity Commission. A written report was also received from the

Joint Liturgical Consultation in New Zealand. Among the resolutions of this meeting were:

1. The English Language Liturgical Consultation seeks to assist in bringing about an international ecumenical lectionary.
2. The Consultation invites its member associations to participate in evaluation of the (1983) 'proposal' and to submit the results of this evaluation to the Consultation on Common Texts.
3. This Consultation invites its member associations to engage in a comparative study of the three lectionaries, Roman, '83 and British, and to bring to the next meeting of this body their responses to this study.[16]

This initiative resulted in a further step, taken at the next meeting of ELLC in Brixen, Italy in 1987:

The ELLC wishes to encourage and facilitate the development of an international ecumenical lectionary. It recognizes the *Common Lectionary* of the CCT as the basis from which work toward this lectionary should be carried forward. The ELLC requests that, in addition to receiving as part of its consultation on the lectionary submissions from the member associations of the ELLC, the CCT accept as members of its committee on the lectionary one or two delegates from the ELLC.[17]

This latter decision was facilitated as the Revd Canon Dr Donald Gray of Westminster Abbey and the Joint Liturgical Group began attending the North American Consultation's Lectionary Task Force meetings in New York.

More recent developments in this widening conversation concerning a universal weekly eucharistic lectionary have included the opening of conversations between the English Language Liturgical Consultation and the World Council of Churches in Geneva (1993), and the Holy See (1994), as well as increased use of the *Revised Common Lectionary* in Great Britain with the official approval of such bodies as the Churches of England, Scotland and Wales. The Consultation also regularly hosts informational sessions at the biennial Congresses of *Societas Liturgica*, which have resulted in expressions of interest from other language groups in Europe and Asia, including Korea.

Reflecting on this extraordinary history of the last three decades, one Roman Catholic participant, Msgr Frederick McManus, has commented:

... today's situation is already a remarkable sign of ecumenical convergence. That we can hear God's word in a pattern substantially common is a clear blessing for pastoral ecumenical activity. It may simply be in the common recognition that we share week by week in the hearing of God's word according to a common or very similar pattern. It may be in the ways in which preachers and people explore the Scriptures together. It may be in quiet ecumenism of one less barrier between the Churches – and this in the blessed area of the inspired Scriptures celebrated in the Sunday Eucharist.[18]

CHAPTER 2

Using the *Revised Common Lectionary*

In undertaking to use the *Revised Common Lectionary* it is important to be aware of the internal structural assumptions by which the lections were chosen and arranged; this is especially true for anyone who would preach on the basis of this three-year sequence of pericopes from both Testaments. All lectionary systems, however, function in a number of ways quite other than for the purpose of preaching. Those other functions are worthy of mention here, including that of preaching, before the basic principles of selection and arrangement are described.

Although probably not exhaustive, a list of six such functions may be made, though they are not necessarily placed in order of importance. The list may, however, reflect a certain historical process by the Church in her liturgical use of the Scriptures.

The *first* of these functions is suggested by Justin Martyr's description of the early Roman liturgy:

On Common Ground

'The memoirs of the apostles or the writings of the prophets are read for as long as time permits.'[19] In a much later day (as noted earlier), the *Westminster Directory of Worship* (1645) said very much the same thing:

> It is requisite that all the Canonical books be read over in order, that the people may be better acquainted with the whole Body of the Scriptures: And ordinarily, where the Reading in either testament endeth on one Lord's day, it is to begin the next.[20]

Paragraph 35 of the Vatican Council's *Sacrosanctum concilium states*: 'In sacred celebrations a more ample, more varied, and more suitable reading from Sacred Scripture should be restored.' The Introduction to the Second Edition of the Roman *Ordo* (1981) in paragraph 59 says, 'The decision on revising the Lectionary for Mass was to draw up and edit a single, rich, and full Order of Readings that would be in complete accord with the intent and prescriptions of the Council.' This first function therefore might be described as 'full and catechetical' in form and intent.

The *second* function can be described as 'Preaching'. Thus Justin Martyr adds, 'When the reader has finished, the president in a discourse urges and invites [us] to the imitation of these noble things.'[21] And we may remember also that 'For Luther, the emphasis was on preaching...The lectionary for the mass was above all motivation for preaching, for proclamation which actualizes the Word. Luther was suspicious of the mere reading of scripture which was not followed by preaching.'[22] Thus also paragraph 52 of *Sacrosanctum concilium*:

By means of the homily the mysteries of the faith and the guiding principles of the Christian life are expounded from the sacred text during the course of the liturgical year. The homily, therefore, is to be highly esteemed as part of the liturgy itself. In fact at those Masses which are celebrated on Sundays and holidays of obligation, with the people assisting, it should not be omitted except for a serious reason.[23]

Although much of this would seem to need no repetition for much of the Protestant community, the glaring exception is on those Sundays when the 'infrequent' Eucharist is included. On those days, in some Presbyterian churches one will be treated not to a sermon or homily but a brief devotional snippet called the 'communion meditation'. And from other traditions one has often heard, 'Since we're celebrating Communion we don't need a sermon, do we?' And what of that much-loved Anglican tradition of 'the eight o'clock communion' where neither sermon nor hymn intrude? This function of the lectionary, therefore, though it is not always observed, is for preaching.

The *third* function of the lectionary is for the observance of feasts, festivals and seasons. This is the origin, in all probability, of *lectio selecta* as an important principle of lectionary formation. We need only think of the fourth-century pilgrim Egeria's appreciation of the fact that during the Holy Week liturgies in Jerusalem, 'the psalms and antiphons they use are always appropriate... Everything is suitable, appropriate, and relevant to what is being done.'[24] And one may recall the seriousness of a Luther or a Cranmer as to the relationship between lectionary and calendar, a feature which is not as significant to the Calvinist of the sixteenth century, much less to the Puritan of the seventeenth century.

This fact renders the more curious a recent development among Protestant and Free churches in the English-speaking world, namely, the growing use by these churches of the classic Christian calendar which begins at Advent and continues through the season of Pentecost or Trinity. That this calendar should come into use is of course a happy development, though not at all consonant with the Puritan background of many of these churches. What is curious is that the festivals and seasons of the year have come into use with no thought as to how the classic lectionaries celebrate and define them. Thus the traditional link between lectionary and calendar has been broken. More recently these traditions have all been reminded anew of the importance of that link by Professor Thomas Talley's ground-breaking work on the origins of the liturgical year.[25]

The *fourth* function of a lectionary has to do with a matter that is somewhat more difficult to define very precisely. This has to do with the way in which the Church's reading of Holy Scripture through the year is also shaped by cultural, climatic, seasonal and ethnic realities. Of course, the debate about the origins of Christmas and Epiphany has always turned on this kind of question. But Professor Talley's scholarship has opened up new questions at this point.

This same sort of issue is well documented by the eminent British liturgical scholar, the late John Gunstone, in an address at the 1981 Paris Congress of *Societas Liturgica* in which he refers to 'the rhythms in which most people spend their lives and the effect these have on liturgical observances'.[26] He continues, 'The rhythms of contemporary life for the majority of English people are dominated by bank holidays, school terms and week-ends.'[27] This reality, he observes, seriously contradicts the ecclesial 'logic' of the traditional Christian calendar in that it often removes many of the faithful from their parishes on the great festivals of Christmas, Easter and Pentecost! Therefore, between the third function of feasts, festivals and seasons and the fourth function of cultural, climatic, seasonal, and ethnic factors there appears to be a certain pattern of contradiction, at least in Great Britain. But of course exactly the same problem now afflicts the weekly festival of the Lord's Day, certainly in North America, as the weekend becomes a time for travel, and Sunday a day for recreation and sporting fixtures. Thus the Roman Church has wisely instituted Saturday evening Vigil Masses, which are often the most widely attended.

This functioning of lectionary and calendar becomes problematic in another way, since cultural and civic observances have a tendency to displace either continuous or selected pericopes. Gunstone speaks of the 'aliturgical' feasts of Mothering Sunday on Lent 4 and Harvest Thanksgiving on a Sunday in September or early October, while pastors in the United States struggle annually with Mothers' Day (which sometimes conflicts with Pentecost), Memorial Day Sunday, Thanksgiving Sunday and the 4th of July weekend.

Lurking behind this (dys)functionality of the lectionary is an enormous 'prior question' which Gunstone did hint at elliptically. That is the unquestioned way in which the Christian Church's liturgical parents, the Jews, embraced the whole cycle of the natural order of annual seasons, harvests, night and day, and the historical order of exile and return, and made of these things their festivals and seasons. How can the Church, in its understanding of law and grace, construct that kind of

Hagaddah? Luther, Calvin and the other major reformers of the sixteenth century were quite clear that evangelical freedom overrides even such institutions as Sabbaths and Festivals. Does this argue for or against the liturgical, lectionary celebration of civic, cultural, seasonal or natural occasions?

The *fifth* function of the lectionary has to do with its immediate context, the liturgy of the day. The Introduction to the Second Edition of the Roman *Ordo* (1981), paragraph 10 reads as follows: 'It can never be forgotten, therefore, that the divine word read and proclaimed by the Church in the liturgy has as its one goal the sacrifice of the New Covenant and the banquet of grace, that is, the Eucharist.'

The reading and proclamation of the Word of God happens as part of a temporal, dramatic, communal event which is propelled by many dynamics of memory, hope, aesthetics, inter-personal relationships and inner-personal trauma. The reading and hearing of pericopes from the Old and New Testaments in the liturgy is clearly a dramatic, ceremonial and evocative event. Thus, such considerations as the quality of public proclamation, the physical appearance of the sacred books, the placing of the lectern, the use of vestments and incense, and the complementarity of music, are critical. Unhappily, all of this is severely threatened, or at least compromised, by the use in many Protestant congregations of pew Bibles, just as Missalettes distract the Catholic worshipper from the 'action' of the Mass and proper participation therein.

Another way of stating this function is to speak of the 'doxological' character of the lectionary. Some would oppose this function to what has already been defined as the catechetical, or 'full' use of Scripture in worship. The Liturgy of the Word at the Easter Vigil, however, would seem to put to rest such a sharp disjunction. But an issue remains, because just as the full use of Scripture would seem to argue for lengthy pericopes, the doxological use of Scripture would seem to argue for brief pericopes. One way of resolving the matter is to recover the Daily Office with its more continuous and fulsome reading of Holy Writ, thus reserving the Sunday Eucharist for shorter, selected passages appropriate to the calendar with its festivals, or simply the Sunday solemnity. Possible as this resolution might seem, it has to be concluded that it is probably not possible for the average worshipper. The other way to work at this problem is by reference to the second function, that of preaching. That means that preaching, liturgical preaching, must be understood not only as teaching, which it is, but also as proclamation, 'proclaiming the Lord's death until he comes'.

This is the point at which the post-Scripture/ sermon liturgical 'moment' needs to be brought into play: the Profession of Faith and the General Intercessions. Oddly, in both Protestant and

Catholic liturgies, these moments seem strangely anti-climactic whereas they should carry the homily precisely into its doxological fulfilment. How could that be done? Perhaps for instance, the Profession should be couched in a more ceremonial or musical medium, or the Intercessions could be freed on the Protestant side from an interminable, oratorical clerical monologue sometimes known as the 'pastoral prayer', and on the Catholic side from undisciplined effusions, by a careful relating of the petitions being offered to the language and spirit of the lectionary and homily. *Ordo* (1981) puts this well:

> Enlightened by God's word and in a sense responding to it, the assembly of the faithful prays in the general intercessions as a rule for the needs of the universal Church and the local community, for the salvation of the world and those oppressed by any burden, and for special categories of people.[28]

The problematic aspect of this doxological use of lectionary functioning is that it might overwhelm the kerygmatic and proclamatory function, and at the same time, subordinate Word to eucharistic liturgy. That is a development which Roman Catholics probably do not wish to repeat and which Protestants (and Anglicans?) would undertake at their peril.

The *sixth* and perhaps final of these functions can

be described as 'Historical and Ecumenical Witness'. There are historic traditions in both continuous and selected lectionaries. There are rich and ancient traditions of certain lessons on certain feasts and certain continuities in certain seasons. The German Lutheran *Ordo* is obviously very careful to keep in use the ancient readings of the Western rite so as to keep that continuity alive, including the wonderful musical commentary thereon produced by J. S. Bach in his well-regulated church music for organ and voice. Christians do expect certain readings at certain times. That is to be conservative in the best sense of the word.

Another side of this historical continuity is its ecumenical dimension. The Church of Jesus Christ has not always been quite as divided and fragmented as it is today, and has been for far too many days. The lectionary is one vital way to keep in touch with those better ancient days where certain texts were heard ecumenically, that is, throughout the whole inhabited earth, or at least throughout the whole jurisdiction of the bishop. The table of the Word must be a place of unity and accord. And it may just be that in our time, unity at that table may well become the opening to that more complete unity at the table of the Eucharist. That is certainly the witness of countless Christians in countries where the Roman system now is mirrored in Protestant and Anglican churches by their use of the *Revised Common Lectionary*. Just as the Bible is the Church's one and agreed source of revelation, so also might its liturgical use become a sign of its oneness in hope.

With this listing of the various functions which any lectionary system serves, it is now possible to turn to the inner structure of this particular system to see how its patterns of selection work.

The *Revised Common Lectionary* and its earlier edition of 1983 continue the pattern of the Roman *Lectionary for Mass* of 1969. The 1992 revision follows the basic calendar of the Western Church and provides for a three-year cycle of three readings on each Lord's Day.

Except for occasional changes, the *Revised Common Lectionary* accepts the *cornerstone* of the Roman lectionary: the semi-continuous reading of the three synoptic Gospels over a three-year period. The Roman pattern connects the first (Old Testament) reading with the gospel for the Sundays after Epiphany and Pentecost. These Old Testament passages are perceived as a parallel, a contrast, or as a type leading to its fulfilment in the gospel. The *Revised Common Lectionary*, however, provides two approaches to the first reading for the Sundays after Pentecost: one set of Old Testament readings continues the Roman lectionary pattern, while the other, the preferred one, offers a series of semi-continuous passages, allowing a larger variety of particular Old Testament themes to be presented. This latter approach has characterized this system ever since the publication of the *Common Lectionary* in 1983. The Introduction to that proposal describes this approach as follows:

Thus it was determined to use the Sundays following Pentecost for semi-continuous reading of the Old Testament as well and by the choice of books to retain a broad, though not necessarily week-by-week, 'harmony' with the gospels. In this way the typological principle was loosened but not abandoned and the semi-continuous principle was reinforced...Although no particular attempt was made to correlate the Old Testament narrative passages with the gospel lesson week-by-week it was the judgment of the revision committee that to read the pentateuchal material along with Matthew (Year A) was to respect that Gospel's own preoccupation, as also is the case with the pairing of David and Mark (Year B), and the prophets and Luke (Year C). Where individual Wisdom or prophetic lessons were chosen which were not particularly sequential week-after-week, then 'harmony' with the gospel or epistle was a criterion of selection.[29]

The effect of this structural 'shift' from the Roman to the Revised list is to create a unique situation during the Sundays after Pentecost in Ordinary Time wherein there are three separate 'tracks' week to week: continuous readings from the Gospel of the year, and also from the Epistles, and semi-continuous readings from the Old Testament. (The Ordinary Time Sundays from Epiphany to Lent retain a week-to-week 'linkage' of gospel and Old Testament, although the epistle set is continuous and for that reason, thematically independent.)

The importance of this observation is to alert preachers to the fact that after Pentecost, using the semi-continuous Old Testament set means that there will *not* be a thematic unity among the three lessons (the psalm being considered simply as a response to the Old Testament lection), nor therefore should such be forced. In response to the inevitable question raised by preachers in this writer's hearing – namely, why should they read all three if only one is to be used homiletically – one can only refer to the various other functions of lections (other than homiletical) as listed above.

During the more festal seasons of Advent – Christmas – Epiphany 1 and Lent – Easter – Day of Pentecost/Trinity, on the other hand, the Roman and Revised tables are of one accord in selecting all three lessons for their coherence both seasonally and in terms of an integration of the Gospel for the year and the Fourth Gospel.

During these particular seasons certain thematic decisions have been made which should be noted, as follows.

(1) In Advent (in all three years) the first Sunday

always highlights apocalyptic literature; the second
and third Sundays recount the prophetic ministry of
John the Baptist, which is also apocalpytic; and the
fourth Sunday (often erroneously called Christmas
Sunday) speaks of the Annunciation. This makes it
quite clear that Advent is preoccupied primarily
with the Second Coming of the Lord rather than
the First (which should raise some sort of question
concerning the widespread devotional custom of
lighting an Advent Wreath as part of the entry rite).

(2) At the transition from Christmas to Epiphany,
it is considered preferable to transfer a weekday
Epiphany festival to the previous Sunday so as not
to miss the baptismal festival on the Sunday after.
Moreover, the Transfiguration pericopes may be
used either on the last Sunday after Epiphany or
on the Second Sunday in Lent, according to various
traditions.

(3) The pericopes for the Sundays of Lent (in all
three years) anticipate the Resurrection event and as
such are not penitential, which is why they are not
counted as part of the forty days of Lent. The
readings for Year A are particularly appropriate if
the parish is engaged in a catechumenal programme
which will culminate in baptism/confirmation at
Easter. For this reason the Roman Catholic Church
has given permission to use those readings in any of
the three lectionary years.

(4) The Sundays during the Great Fifty Days of
Easter continue the resurrection proclamation in

the following ways: (a) the gospel readings are the resurrection narratives from all four Gospels; (b) the first reading replaces Old Testament pericopes with readings from the book of Acts, an ancient tradition, which reflects the conviction that the earliest and most impressive witness to the reality of resurrection is the life of the Christian community as recounted in that second volume of St Luke; and (c) the New Testament (second) readings are drawn alternately from the Johannine epistles or from the book of Revelation, signifying the twin ways in which Christians themselves continue to witness to the resurrection, namely by their mutual love and their corporate worship.

(5) An alternative Old Testament passage is provided for Pentecost Day, as also for Easter Day, with the provision for moving the Acts passage to the place of the second reading.

With these clarifications concerning structural and thematic assumptions we may now turn more specifically to the implications for the preacher of using the *Revised Common Lectionary*. In another place[30] this commentator has identified five such implications.

Sundays as Sequential – Narrative Preaching

Perhaps the single most revolutionary result of using the *Revised Common Lectionary*, for churches which have never used a lectionary as

well as for churches whose lectionaries were based
in the Western, Latin tradition, will be the experience of Sunday as the occasion for hearing a
sequence of biblical passages. It could be said that
the history of lectionaries in the Western Church
has seen a gradual shift from *lectio continua* (as in
the Synagogue and the early Roman church) to
lectio selecta. The continuing occasion for this
shift was calendrical, in that the Sunday calendar
came to include more annual dates, in contrast to
the earlier pattern wherein the *Pascha* was the only
annual festival (and that only after the Council of
Nicaea) with perhaps Epiphany in the East (also a
fixed date) and later Christmas in the West (a fixed
date). Thus, as the sixteenth-century Reformers
perceived, the principal recurring festival of the
Church was in fact, the Lord's Day. Hence there
was no reason to interrupt the course reading of 'the
memoirs of the apostles or the writings of the
prophets'. It was only as the annual calendar
became more elaborate in the cycles of Sundays
around Christmas and *Pascha* that the *continua*
pattern was interrupted by a *selecta* principle. This
of course had probably been done even in the
Synagogue on Sabbaths proximate to the *Pascha*
and the major Holy Days.

At the same time, as the first millennium drew to
its close, other calendrical cycles, such as the
sanctorale and Marian festivals, imposed their
own selected pericopes on the Sunday sequence.

Thus, by the time of the Reformation of the six-teenth century, continuous reading had disappeared altogether, and even had it not, the linguistic barrier would have rendered it unintelligible. Further, with the celebration of Mass, which might have secured the uniqueness of the Lord's Day festival, having become a daily event, it was insufficient to suggest to the faithful that the Lord's Day, as a recurring weekly event, formed its own calendar with a combination of proper and ordinary elements having to do with the regular *anamnesis* of the death and resurrection of the Lord. The increasing secularization of the Lord's Day and the increase in the number of Holy Days only reinforced the loss of that day as a continuing sequence of celebrations.

It was probably John Calvin, with his extensive knowledge of the early Fathers, who most clearly understood the symmetry between the Lord's Day as the primary Christian festival, the Lord's Supper, and the course reading of Scripture on that day. Thus his reading and preaching of the Scriptures on the Lord's Day reverted to *lectio continua*, being interrupted only by the annual festivals of Christmas, Easter and Pentecost. Indeed, when thwarted in his attempts to recover a weekly eucharistic celebration or even a monthly schedule he turned to those great festivals as the eucharistic days, a strategy which even his own ecclesial descendants in Scotland and North America have never under-stood with their strict 'quarterly' pattern. Even the

Puritan anti-Prayer Book *Directory for Worship* of the Westminster Assembly (1645) recommended course reading from the Old and New Testaments.

With the publication by the Holy See of *Ordo lectionum Missae* in 1969, the Western rite at last returned to this principle in large measure. Thus the Synoptic Gospels are read in their entirety, week by week, year by year, resorting to a *selecta* pattern only for Lent – Easter – Day of Pentecost and Advent – Christmas – Epiphany 1. Thus also the Pauline and Pastoral epistles are read the same way during Ordinary Time after Pentecost. And with the *Revised Common Lectionary* (and its immediate predecessor, the *Common Lectionary*) the *continua* principle was applied to the First Reading in Ordinary Time after Pentecost. That is why, as noted above, the *Revised Common Lectionary* provides an alternate set of Old Testament pericopes for this period in the Year which more nearly accords with the Roman 'typological' system as found also in the *Lutheran Book of Worship* (1978) and the Episcopal *Book of Common Prayer* (1979). It can be reported, however, that as of this writing it has been announced in the Consultation on Common Texts (North America) that both the Evangelical Lutheran Church in America and the Episcopal Church in the United States have officially approved the *Revised Common Lectionary* as an option to the tables now printed in their own books, although the Lutheran

Church recommended the 'typological' option for the Sundays after Pentecost.

But what does this recovery of *lectio continua* mean for preaching? Interestingly the most important points apply equally to traditional lectionary-using churches and to those which have not done so until this past decade. One suspects that the significance of this recovery is only now becoming clear. This recovery requires that the preacher, and the hearers, need to think about a Sunday-to-Sunday sequence of pericopes. Put another way, the scriptural context for Sunday's sermon is 'horizontally' determined rather than 'vertically'. The consonance of lessons is week-to-week rather than lesson-to-lesson on a given Sunday, at least in Ordinary Time after Pentecost. This makes the often heard complaint that lectionary preaching doesn't provide opportunity for series sermons quite ironic since the *continua* principle builds that possibility into the heart of proclamation. The difference from the popular assumption is that the series consists of the Scriptures themselves rather than some artificial construct such as 'Great Personages in the Bible', 'The Apostles' Creed in Paul's Letters', and so on. This places the preacher and people in a new relationship to the recurring Lord's Day. It assumes a fairly stable, regular congregation and means that preacher and people must undertake the kind of preparation for the Lord's Day through the week which may well, as a side effect, bring back to

Protestant homes the daily scrutiny of the Scriptures. For the preacher it certainly means that there
will have to be a more careful study of biblical books
in use than was ever the case when one could skip
about one's favourite books from week to week.
This professor's students are counselled each year
in Advent, or shortly before, to purchase and famil-
iarize themselves with the latest and best commentaries on the Gospel for the year. The same could be
said for the epistles to be read after Pentecost.
Further, it is to be hoped that by the end of each of
the three-year cycles the congregation itself will
have a fairly clear picture of the unique character-
istics of the Synoptic Gospel for that year.

This is emphatically not to turn the Lord's Day
celebration into a liturgical 'Bible study' session, as
some have criticized. It is simply to include in one's
preaching the sort of contextualization which is
essential to understanding the pericopes as the
bases for sermons and homilies.

What is equally difficult for many preachers to
accept is the above-mentioned fact that for fully half
the calendar year the three readings for the day may
well have no thematic coherence. Even the most
sophisticated series of lectionary commentaries find
it hard not to find some sort of inter-relationship
among the three (and some would say, four, since
they fail to grasp the unique function of the psalm
for the day as a sung response to the First Reading).
Worse, whether guided by these commentaries or

their own traditional concept of preaching, some preachers, realizing that there is no inner relationship thematically, will simply preach three rather brief and simplistic sermonettes! Evidence of this sort of assumption often surfaces with the question as to why, if one is not going to use all three lessons in the homily, does one read them at all. That is to say, in certain traditions the assumption has been that one only reads from the Scriptures for the purpose of preaching. The corollary of this assumption is its undoing (certainly in a Protestant context), namely, that what once was called 'dumb reading', that is, reading without commentary, cannot possibly be edifying for the people of God. Surely this evidences a kind of Protestant 'priestcraft' which is thoroughly inappropriate precisely in that tradition. One recalls a line from a much-loved hymn of William Cowper: 'God is His own interpreter, and He will make it plain.'

There is, however, a way to counter this sort of challenge and also to respect the *continua* principle. That is, to preface all readings by the briefest kind of *incipit* ('introduction') whereby the community is reminded of the textual context of each lesson, whether or not it is to be used homiletically. In conclusion then, we can posit the proposition that the *Revised Common Lectionary*, properly used, will require of the preacher a new level of biblical background and of the people a new level of concentration that will carry over from one Sunday to the next. One needn't belabour the deeper implications of this exercise for a theological description of the character of the liturgical assembly as the principal place for continuing catechesis and deepening in faith wherein the ever-changing biblical material, in sequence, is paired with the ever-constant eucharistic celebration.

Scripture as its Own Context

This point is obviously closely related to the previous paragraphs. The particular issue that needs attention here has to do with the questions of literary genre and the formation of the various books of the Bible in relation to their communities and the canonization process. Here we are taking aboard at least two fairly recent schools of biblical study: on the one hand the 'canon criticism' school that addresses the historical process by which given Christian communities formed and canonized their books, and on the other hand the 'literary historical' school that reads the Scriptures in terms of their relationship to known literary forms of their times.

One might observe that what these two schools of thought seek is actually to describe the formation of the canonical books as 'lectionaries in the making'. The goal of these two schools of study is to provide us with a sensitivity as to how given books were formed, in the context of their particular communities and of literary conventions of their own times. In the same way, the goal of both the *Ordo lectionum Missae* and the *Revised Common Lectionary* is to provide contemporary communities with a form of proclamation which takes account, on a weekly basis, of these factors in order to re-form those historic communities in the present day, the homily being the operative literary form. In this regard one thinks of the suggestive small book by Raymond E. Brown, *The Churches the Apostles Left Behind*,[31] or James A. Sanders' *Torah and Canon*,[32] *Canon and Community*,[33] and *God Has A Story Too*.[34]

These schools of biblical criticism return the study and proclamation of the Scriptures to their original, communal, ecclesial context in prospect, just as the use of a lectionary whose basis is largely *continua* and whose *selecta* Sundays relate to the community's recurring annual festivals do the same in retrospect. Moreover, with Scripture as its own context ('interpreter') the liturgical assembly is constantly being introduced to what the late Karl Barth called 'the strange new world within the Bible'. As he puts it: 'within the Bible there is a strange, new world, the world of God...'[35] And again, 'There is a river in the Bible that carries us away, once we have entrusted our destiny to it – away from ourselves to the sea.'[36] Here, too, we discover a powerful symmetry between the Liturgy of the Word and the Liturgy of the Table, between the spoken language of scripture and sermon and the prayed and gestured language of the Table, the 'two tables'.

In this regard it is possible to think of the homily itself as a particular literary form, closely related to the community within which it occurs. A sermon needn't always be hortatory, or didactic or narrative – though it well may be, depending on the scriptural material for the day. A sermon might also be lyrical, poetic, hymnic, euchological or meditative. One has only to dip into the homilies of the ancient Fathers to discover this, and how interesting that they were often, if not always, working with a *continua* principle. That is, of course, the reason that the *Revised Common Lectionary* reads books such as Epistles, Synoptic Gospels, Acts and Old Testament history in a continuous or semi-continuous way, whereas the Fourth Gospel is used in a 'selected' way in relationship to the Christian calendar just as its literary structure seems to be related to the Jewish calendar.

At a time when the world of the Bible is increasingly strange, both because of increasing biblical illiteracy and the increasingly secular and even violent character of contemporary society, the preacher must be able to find a way for the people of God into the world of God. And a preacher, Catholic or Protestant, who works carefully with such a lectionary system as we now have available, will find that the world of God just might make more sense than the 'worlds in collision' of our times, which seem always to be either exploding or imploding. As Luther's hymn proclaims, 'That word above all earthly powers, no thanks to them, abideth...God's truth abideth still; His kingdom is forever.'

Lectionary and Calendar

We now turn our attention to the guidance the *Revised Common Lectionary* provides for the preacher in those festal seasons wherein the principle of selection is not *continua* but *selecta*: Advent and Christmas (including Epiphany and Epiphany 1) and Lent and Easter (including Pentecost/Trinity). Once again we must take note of the different directions from which preachers in various traditions will come to the *Revised Common Lectionary* Clerics of the so-called 'liturgical churches', such as Roman Catholic, Lutheran and Anglican, will be quite used to the consonance of season and lectionary, even though (as we will note shortly) the lections chosen may well require certain changes in their traditional understanding of these seasons. On the other hand, clerics of the so-called 'free churches' have either paid no attention to the classic annual calendar or – and this is of considerable importance – have begun to celebrate the cycles of Christmas and Easter, simply as seasons, without regard to the defining character of the day's lections. Curiously, this has been the pattern in many North American Protestant communities. Thus these seasons of Advent/Christmas/Epiphany and Lent/

37

Easter/Pentecost have come to be observed without proper attention to the way in which classical Western lectionaries have *defined their meaning*. On the face of it, this is a strange and even contradictory way for Protestants to shape their worship, that is, by reference to a set of seasons without regard to the way in which the biblical selections for those seasons define them. This has resulted in all manner of anomalies such as the Fourth Sunday of Advent being designated 'Christmas Sunday', and, in one church's Ministers' Daily Diary, the Sunday after Christmas being designated 'The Fifth Sunday in Advent'. At Epiphany, the Magi would often displace the Baptism of the Lord depending on where in the week 6 January occurred. In the Paschal cycle a penitential mood has pervaded all the Lenten Sundays without it being noticed that those Sundays are not even counted as part of Lent in that they anticipate Easter, not Good Friday (a misunderstanding which was not altogether absent from the more liturgical churches and which has only been corrected even there by the Gospels and related pericopes for Lent in the three-year systems). Also, among the free churches there was little practice of a *season* of Easter – the Great Fifty Days – and as a result Pentecost was a detached, free-standing festival which became 'the Birthday of the Church' (as though Christ had not called his Church into being at the moment of the calling of the Twelve!)

Using the Revised Common Lectionary

With the emerging use of the *Revised Common Lectionary*, however, preachers were jolted into a re-definition of much of these festal times *on the basis of* the biblical pericopes; a curious twist, in that a Catholic-derived, biblical system was needed to call Protestant preaching to a more evangelical use of the classic calendar! Thus it suddenly became clear that Advent had to do not with the First Coming of Christ but the Second. This confusion is further compounded by the cultural pressure to begin singing Christmas carols as early as the First Sunday in Advent, such that one even hears references to 'this Christmas season'. And, of course, when the Twelve Days of Christmas are begun on 25 December, the worshipping community – like its surrounding culture – is weary of the whole thing and has little interest in further festivity, except for welcoming the Magi at Epiphany. As already mentioned, the same corrective has been administered concerning the Sundays in Lent by virtue of the biblical plan of the three-year cycle which anticipates Easter rather than Good Friday. A further revision of (Protestant) homiletical tradition is administered by these lectionary systems at the newly-designated Passion/Palm Sunday moment, which in much of Free church practice was devoted exclusively to the Triumphal Entry, the Passion being left to the days of Holy Week (which are increasingly poorly attended, and celebrated in sometimes embarrassingly literalistic and dramatic fashion) so that the preacher never has an opportunity to 'preach the Passion'. Finally, the Sunday pericopes for the Sundays after Easter now remind the most careless preacher that the Resurrection celebration does not end with Easter Day but in fact *begins* with it.

Thus it has come about that this ecumenical lectionary system has at last reminded the universal Church that it is the Bible that shapes the calendar and preaching, and not the calendar that shapes the preaching. For those who have eyes to see and ears to hear, this is the clear message of Professor Thomas Talley's magisterial study, *The Origins of the Liturgical Year*. It is precisely this mix of continuous and selected biblical pericopes that gives the calendar of the Christian community whatever shape and evangelical significance it is to have for the people of God.

Preacher and Text

For preachers from ecclesial traditions which have never prescribed a lectionary the current situation requires a totally new way of thinking about their relation to the biblical texts. Oddly, this new way is in a direction which would seem to be axiomatic for Protestants, but which in fact has certainly not been. Thus the preacher now no longer chooses the preaching texts; they choose the preacher. The way this is most often expressed is the complaint that 'There's nothing about these texts that "turns me on".' To express this situation in a more sophisticated way, one might observe that for the preacher to live with the luxury of choosing the weekly preaching texts is to run the grave risk of reducing the Canon of Holy Scripture to those books and pericopes that are congenial with the preacher's own theological preoccupations or, worse, with the limitations of the preacher's seminary study of the Bible. Most preachers who take on the responsibility of working consistently with the lectionary soon become painfully aware of how little of the Canon they were using when the principle of selection was entirely their own. Underlying this reality, of course, is the larger and more significant issue of the inspiration of Holy Scripture. In Calvinism this has been expressed by the doctrinal affirmation that the Scriptures only become the Word of God by virtue of the 'inward testimony of the Holy Spirit'.

There is, of course, a more problematic side to this laudable practice of placing oneself, as preacher, at the disposal of the lectionary table and that is the danger that one abandons altogether any creative energy in making the lectionary's choices one's own. This can result either in a careless and forced attempt to define a common theme – even when such does not exist, as in the Sundays after Pentecost – or, as mentioned above, a lifeless and perfunctory series of three (or four!) brief comments on the texts of the day. This is why lectionary preaching requires that the preacher plan well ahead as to

41

which of the biblical sequences are to be followed, for instance, after Pentecost. It is also doubly important that the preacher has a minimal understanding of the lectionary's own principles and plan, in order that the selections made by the lectionary be clear to him or her well before the sermon is planned. More importantly, perhaps, is that the preacher then brings his or her own critical faculties to bear on any given Sunday's selections, as to whether the lectionary's choices might have to be emended or edited. Thus, although the use of a lectionary can be of vital assistance to the preacher, one must guard against a certain homiletical laziness since the principal choices for the sermon have already been made. It could be said that the preacher is only using the lectionary well when the sermonic work is *harder* than when the preacher was choosing the texts week by week.

Preaching as Participatory

Perhaps one of the most important possibilities at the parish level that the use of the *Revised Common Lectionary* provides – and this is not altogether different from using any other lectionary system – is that it becomes possible to invite the parish community to enter into a regular discipline, along with their preacher, of study and preparation for Sunday's Liturgy of the Word. As was not possible when the preacher chose the texts on a week-by-week basis, often sometimes during the week just before their use, it is now possible to alert the congregation in advance (at least at the previous week's assembly) as to what lessons will occur on the following Sunday. This in turn suggests that regular lectionary study groups might be convened wherein the pastor can work in advance, *with the faithful*, to prepare the homily. This could also be conjoined with training sessions for lay readers, for it is often the case that only when one takes the time to proclaim the pericopes audibly that certain subtleties and nuances begin to appear.

Another aspect of parish participation has to do with the proper integration of various elements of the parish liturgy and life, such as music and Christian education. Use of the *Revised Common Lectionary* makes possible that which lectionary-using churches have always known, namely, that it is possible for the parish musician(s) to plan ahead regarding choral and instrumental music which will relate to the biblical texts for the day. With the publication of the 1983 and 1992 systems a vast publishing activity has developed to point the way for such integration on a weekly basis. The same may be said of curricula now being produced for use in the church schools and adult education programmes. These programmes need no longer be tangential or even totally unrelated to the liturgical and homiletical life of the community, but rather supportive thereof.

Another way in which preaching may become more participatory has to do with the widespread ecumenical acceptance of this system. The English Language Liturgical Consultation continues to hear of wider and wider use of this system, not only in the English-speaking world of Great Britain, North America, Australia, New Zealand and South Africa, but also in other language groups, as in Scandanavia and Korea, and in many mission situations in the Third World. This use in all these places is by Anglicans and quite a few Protestant bodies. Further, the close relationship between the *Revised Common Lectionary* and the Roman Lectionary means that throughout the world many churches in hundreds of thousands of local situations are reading the Scriptures together on the Lord's Day. This has already resulted in the formation of clerical lectionary study groups throughout the world and especially in those places where ecumenical co-operation is an accepted and acceptable experience. This represents a fulfilment of the fondest hopes of the framers first of the *Common Lectionary* and now of the *Revised Common Lectionary*. One might be allowed the vision that as separated ecclesial communities begin to participate *together* in the weekly, homiletical study of the Holy Scriptures, the Lord's priestly prayer is coming to fruition: 'I have given them your word...Sanctify them in the truth; your word is truth' (John 17:14, 17).

CHAPTER 3

The *Revised Common Lectionary*: The Underlying Ecumenical Hermeneutic

Almost thirty years after the publication by the Roman Catholic Church of its revised, three-year Lectionary for Mass, a Protestant scholar of lectionary and liturgical matters, Fritz West, has brought forth an important study of the relationship between this Roman model and its later Protestant and ecumenically-conceived descendants of 1983 and 1992. His book is entitled *Scripture and Memory: The Ecumenical Hermeneutic of the Three-Year Lectionaries.*[37] It is essential reading for anyone who would use, in a knowledgeable way, either the Roman or the ecumenical system, to say nothing of those who might be inspired to prepare running commentaries on the pericopes of these systems, week by week. This writer and intimate participant in every stage of the preparation of the ecumenical cycle can only confess that

Fritz West has understood the schema and assumptions underlying this effort perhaps even better than those of us who have spent many hours over many years in this undertaking. Further, West has so well identified the discontinuities as well as continuities between the two tables as to have uncovered in a singular way what he calls, an 'ecumenical hermeneutic' implicit in these widely-used guides to the liturgical use of Scripture.

As background for the definition of such an hermeneutic, he describes the two contrasting ways in which Christians have had access to the Bible and its evangelical message, that is, have 'held' it: 'The Catholic liturgical tradition has held Scripture in containers of communal memory; the Protestant liturgical tradition has held it in the Bible. Those two hermeneutical settings interpret the passages from Scripture which they carry in strikingly different ways.'[38] With wonderful concision he points out that 'These lectionaries have combined into a single ecumenical hermeneutic aspects of the historical hermeneutics of the two Western liturgical traditions. Simply stated, they balance the communal memory and the written memory [the Bible] of the Church.'[39]

Another way West describes this pair of approaches to the Bible's story of salvation is by a contrast he speaks of as 'the canonical and the calendrical',[40] the first of which may be understood as to refer to the sweep of the books of the Bible itself in a kind of *heilsgeschichte* by which 'the two Testaments are here bound together by the continuity of God's redemptive intentions',[41] and the second of which may be understood as to refer to the more Christological focus of classic Christian calendars and festivals to be found more on the Catholic side. This is an issue that was raised in 1983 by a pair of essays by this writer and Professor James A. Sanders in a volume on *Social Themes of the Christian Year: A Commentary on the Lectionary*.[42] Sanders was critical of the tendency of a lectionary to 'subordinate the canon to the calendar'[43] and worse, that 'the Old Testament especially is subordinated in Christian lectionaries to at best a supporting role to the New Testament passages chosen'.[44] His proposed solution (in part) was to 'introduce a theocentric perspective in the churches so that God's work in Israel, in Christ, and in the early church can be seen as continuing today'.[45] West notes, in this regard, that Protestant groups, with just such a concern, such as the Lutherans, preferred to define the good news 'as a theological category, theocentric rather than christological'.[46]

Obviously these contrasting hermeneutics find their theological roots and seriousness in the classic dialectic of Protestant and Catholic polemics as between Scripture and tradition. The power of West's analysis, however, is that he finds, precisely in the ecumenical system's schema a significant

47

hermeneutical 'bridge' in the decision by the Consultation on Common Texts to shape its 1983 proposal by re-working the linkage between the gospel and Old Testament pericopes for the Sundays after Pentecost to embrace the Old Testament in a semi-continuous way, precisely the sort of proposal Sanders was hinting at. To explicate this, West defines yet another pair of lectionary analyses, both of which are to be found in the Roman table: 'Fundamentally, the *Lectionary for Mass* relates Scripture mnemonically in two time frames, the one being synchronic and operating on a given Sunday or feast, the other being diachronic and extending across Sundays and feasts.'[47] West notes that Protestantism in North America, after the confusing impact of the historical-critical method and biblical/neo-orthodox theology (referred to early in this volume) was in search of a new hermeneutic which the Roman model seemed to satisfy.[48] His most fascinating insight turns on the meaning of the shift from the Roman ('synchronic') plan for the Old Testament after Pentecost to the more Protestant ('diachronic') plan. He concludes, in a penetrating summary of the ecumenical significance of this step, 'the *Revised Common Lectionary* has arrived at a compelling solution for the balance of the written and communal memories of the Church in the interpretation of Scripture'.[49]

This is impressive testimony to the depth of ecumenical achievement that these developments in lectionary reform have achieved. A close reading of West's subsequent commentary on the major blocks of pericopes in the Roman and Revised tables will bear out his thesis. How very interesting it is that here at the conclusion of a century that has seemingly seen both the rise and the decay of ecumenical efforts, a liturgical-biblical enterprise might already have become the truest and deepest fruit of that impulse. What, then, might be thought of as the next steps?

CHAPTER 4

The Way Ahead: Ecumenical and Multi-Cultural

If one may assume that the present ecumenical acceptance of a three-year system of pericopes for the Lord's Day is firmly enough in place (at least in the English-speaking Protestant and Anglican world) to provide hope for wider use beyond that language group, what might be envisioned as the next steps of even more universal import? Two directions might be sketched.

The first has to do with the possibility that the Holy See of the Roman Catholic Church might see fit to grant 'faculties' to provinces, dioceses or Orders of that church to use the ecumenical table as a suitable alternative to the 1969 Roman document, if only in an experimental way. To this end, the Steering Committee of the English Language Liturgical Consultation made representations to the Congregation of Divine Worship and the Discipline of the Sacraments of the Holy See in May of 1994 at the Vatican City. The Protestant Co-Chair

rehearsed the recent history of lectionary development with particular attention to the *Revised
Common Lectionary* and its relationship to the
Roman table of 1969. He was able to cite the
declaration in 1993 of the Pontifical Biblical Commission entitled 'The Interpretation of the Bible in
the Church', as follows:

The Lectionary, issued at the direction of the
Council (*Sacrosanctum Concilium* Paragraph
35), is meant to allow for a reading of Sacred
Scripture that is 'more abundant, more varied
and more suitable'. In its present state, it only
partially fulfils this goal. Nevertheless, even as it
stands, it has had positive ecumenical results.[50]

The Consultation encouraged the Congregation
'to provide a way or ways for the experimental use
by interested Roman Catholic communities and
Conferences of Bishops, of this attempt of ours, to
bring Christians of all languages and continents in a
visible and audible unity around the table of the
Word of God, the church's primary catechesis and
dogmatic foundation'.[51] A member of this Consultation, present in Rome at that time, has more
recently (November 1997) renewed this appeal.
The Revd Canon Dr Donald Gray, of Westminster
Abbey, addressing the Pontifical Liturgical Institute
at Sant' Anselmo, cited the Consultation's appeal of
1994 and suggested that he found it 'hard to

understand why the Catholic church was dragging its feet, since the new lectionary was substantially the Roman *Ordo lectionis* (sic) *Missae* (1969) in English', and 'that the Vatican's recently published Ecumenical Directory (1993) envisaged this sort of co-operation when it recommended "agreement for common readings for liturgical use"'.[52]

The English Language Liturgical Conference has also recently opened conversations with Roman and Lutheran liturgical authorities at the Liturgical Institute in Trier, Germany and, as reported above, with representatives – Protestant and Catholic – of other linguistic groups at international scholarly gatherings.

The approach to Orthodox and Oriental Orthodox churches has been more difficult and less promising thus far. In Finland, in August 1997, for the first time an official representative of the Ecumenical Patriarchate took part in a Consultation meeting, namely, Fr Ephrem Lash, of Great Britain. This is certainly an important beginning.

Moreover, in 1997 there appeared in *St Vladimir's Theological Quarterly* an interesting and probing article by Fr David Petras, Professor of Liturgy at the Byzantine Catholic Seminary, Pittsburgh, PA (USA), entitled 'The Gospel Lectionary of the Byzantine Church'. He reflects on one of the principal issues involved in Western lectionary reform, in terms quite reminiscent of Vatican II too, as he favours:

open[ing] more of the message of the gospel in a liturgical setting, as a community of faith that feasts on the Word of God, as well as on His body and blood... In order to open more of the gospel for the hearing of the faithful, it will be necessary to make a new arrangement of the continuous reading of the four Gospels while leaving intact those that are intimately bound with the Church year.[53]

He proceeds to a modest set of suggestions which is certainly worth quoting at length:

The gospel sections during the periods of Matthew and Luke could be reformed without distorting the character of the Church year. This would mean the abandonment of the criteria of the original arrangers in favour of the principle of opening as much of the whole Gospel text to the faithful as possible. Western lectionaries are now on a three-year cycle. To extend the reading of the Gospels over more than three years would, it seems to me, make the whole experience more ponderous. The traditional readings for Saturday and Sunday should also be respected and given a special place. Perhaps the best option to examine would be the reading of the present Saturday and Sunday cycles in a period of two years, eliminating the parallel passages that are repeated. The third year can then be composed of those gospel

sections in Mark and John that are not read on
Sunday. Some selection among the pericopes
would be necessary. The decision as to which
readings to be chosen must be made by the authorities of the Churches involved, as the presentation and proclamation of the gospel are their most
important responsibility.[54]

At least, one may hope, common questions are
now being asked, both in the East and West, and, as
has been the case in the West between Catholic and
Protestant churches, perhaps the advent of vernacular liturgy will press some of these questions with a
seriousness not heretofore attempted.

The other direction in which lectionary reform
may want to move has been raised in a number of
ways and places by the growing discussion of such
matters as inculturation, contextualization and
multi-cultural dimensions of the liturgy. As mentioned much earlier in this account, lectionaries
inevitably involve calendars and customs peculiar
to the culture that surrounds the Church in its
diverse geographical and cultural expressions. Certain missionary traditions, such as the Presbyterian
in Korea, found it necessary to reject and suppress
all such manifestations, but of course did not
bring with it much in the way of a formed lectionary and liturgical calendar. Others have found
ways to integrate local observances and customs
within the liturgical traditions brought with them.

But, as discussions among liturgical theologians increasingly indicate, these matters are not simply missionary matters; they are profoundly ecclesiological in their import. Surely the history of the liturgy during the first four or five centuries in the Mediterranean basin and the Graeco-Roman world, moving from Semitic roots, from Hebrew/Aramaic to Greek to Latin, has suggestions along this front that will impact the development, use and reform of lectionary systems. It is certainly not too soon to move on from the monumental progress in this area of the Church's life and mission in this century to horizons yet unglimpsed in another century. For it is the Church's own risen and glorified Lord who is cited as saying, 'See, I am making all things new' (Rev. 21:5, NRSV).

Sola scriptura, sola gratia, sola fidei!

PART TWO

CHAPTER 5

The *Revised Common Lectionary* in the Life of the Church

Part One of this book outlined the story of the development of the *Revised Common Lectionary (RCL)*. Two decades of continuing development, evaluation and revision have led to a major ecumenical accomplishment for the Church. We now have a truly *common* lectionary that is shared widely among numerous churches around the world. The list of participating churches continues to grow as interest in the lectionary spreads.

Producing a common lectionary is one thing. Incorporating the lectionary into the life of the Church is the second major step in the process. In this chapter we will briefly examine the ways in which the *RCL* has been adopted by a sampling of the churches from the list below. In some cases the *RCL* was adopted with very few changes. For example, the Scottish Episcopal Church made no modifications whatsoever. (Though the *RCL* is not mandatory, it is receiving wide use across the church.) On the other hand, the Church of England, after extensive study and evaluation, made some significant adaptations to the lectionary.

The denominations treated in this survey are:

The Presbyterian Church, USA
The Christian Reformed Church in North America
The United Methodist Church
The American Baptist Churches
The Presbyterian Church in Canada
The United Church of Christ
The Evangelical Lutheran Church in America
The Evangelical Lutheran Church in Canada
The United Church of Canada
The Christian Church (Disciples of Christ)
The Episcopal Church
The Anglican Church of Canada
The Church of the Province of Southern Africa (Anglican)
The Church of England
The Anglican Church of Australia
The Scottish Episcopal Church

The Presbyterian Church, USA

The Presbyterian Church (USA) recommends the semi-continuous track during Ordinary Time reflecting its rich Calvinist heritage. The Old Testament has always been emphasized as an integral part of Sunday worship in the Reform tradition. *The Westminster Directory of Public Worship of God* (1645) instructed pastors to read and explicate whole books of the Bible in sequence. Thus the sequential track comes naturally to Presbyterians. The *RCL* has won wide acceptance in the church with about 75 per cent of congregations making regular use of the lectionary.

The Christian Reformed Church in America

The Christian Reformed Church in America, reflecting the same Reformed tradition, makes exclusive use of the semi-continuous track as well. Presently, some 8 per cent of the congregations are using the lectionary, but their new *Psalter Hymnal Handbook* (CRC Publications, 1997) includes the lectionary along with a brief commentary on the use of the lectionary in the congregation. This resource will make the *RCL* more accessible to worship leaders. Reformed practice in the United States is to use one or two biblical texts in a Sunday service.

When psalms are used in worship they are not always sung in the context of the reading of Scripture but may simply be used as a hymn at another place in the service.

On Common Ground

The United Methodist Church

The United Methodist Book of Worship (1992) adopts the semi-continuous track during Ordinary Time. Deuterocanonical readings are replaced with the Old Testament alternatives offered as options in the *RCL*. *The United Methodist Hymnal* does not include all of the psalms cited in the *RCL*, and therefore substitute psalms from the hymnal reflecting the theme of the first reading were selected. Though the use of the lectionary is voluntary, it is widely used by pastors and churches, both for Sunday worship and in daily reading as preparation for or reflection on the word read and proclaimed.

The church publishes numerous resources that aid pastors and worship planners in integrating the lectionary into the life of the congregation, including *The United Methodist Music and Worship Planner* and the *Official United Methodist Program Calendar*.

The American Baptist Churches

The American Baptist Churches regularly includes the *RCL* texts along with the liturgical colours and other resources in their *Annual Planning Calendar/ Directory*. The American Baptist web site also includes the complete *RCL*. The lectionary is widely used across the denomination not only for Sunday worship, but for Bible study and daily devotions as well. The idea of using a lectionary-based curriculum that ties liturgy and education together is finding increased favour in the church.

The Presbyterian Church in Canada

The Presbyterian Church in Canada encourages the use of the *RCL* by including the citations in worship resources, calendars and bulletin materials. Though the semi-continuous Old Testament track is usually followed, occasionally the thematic lection will be suggested for a particular Sunday. *The Book of Psalms: A Worship Resource for Reading or Singing the Psalms with Optional Refrains* (The Presbyterian Church in Canada, 1995) supports the *RCL* by providing a fuller treatment of the liturgical psalms: 'For the one hundred and five psalms in the three-year cycles of the new *Revised Common Lectionary* (1992) this resource provides refrains and a tone for singing the text' (p. v). A three-page table showing all the *RCL* psalm selections provides further support for worship leaders. The *RCL* has won wide acceptance in the church.

The United Church of Christ

The United Church of Christ encourages the use of the *RCL* by publishing lectionary citations in worship books and church calendars. Both semi-continuous and thematically related Old Testament options are cited. The United Church of Christ publishes *The Inviting Word*, a Christian education curriculum based on the *RCL*. The curriculum includes lesson designs for all ages. The vision of the curriculum is that congregational life will increasingly be shaped by the Scripture that is heard Sunday by Sunday and season by season in the lectionary.

> The lectionary is an appropriate guide for organizing biblical content for *The Inviting Word* because it has been and is increasingly used as the focus for congregational worship and preaching. By using the lectionary in Sunday school, in study groups, at home, and in worship, a Bible reading may significantly impact the full life of the congregation.[55]

The desk calendar published by the Stewardship Council of the United Church of Christ is the most official rendering of the lectionary. *The New Century Hymnal* prints a lectionary index of hymns based on the *RCL*. The calendar includes both options with the suggestion that congregations choose either one or the other track for the entire period of Ordinary Time. Since *The Inviting Word* curriculum is based on the *RCL*, the lections are listed in the *Leader's Guide* with both tracks for Ordinary Time included in the lectionary table. One of the three readings or psalm is chosen as a 'focus

Scripture' for each week and is therefore given the fullest treatment. Though most of the Old Testament focus Scriptures are taken from the sequential track during Ordinary Time, there are occasional selections taken from the gospel-related track as well. Thus the church's curriculum may influence the choice of the optional lections used in congregations. The printed bulletin covers and other worship resources produced by the church highlight the curriculum's focus Scripture, further influencing the final choice of lections.

Incidentally, there are two other lectionary-based curricula available on the market today. *Living the Good News*, published by Morehouse Publishing, Harrisburg, Pennsylvania, and *The Whole People of God*, published by Logos Productions, Inc., of Minneapolis, Minnesota. As noted above, basing the congregation's education and overall programme on the *RCL* may have a profound effect on how the lectionary is incorporated into the congregation. The acceptance of the *RCL* by the United Church of Canada was influenced, at least in part, by the growing popularity of *The Whole People of God* among the congregations.

The two-track system of lections allows churches to make their choice reflecting their understanding of the role of the Old Testament in the liturgy.

Several of the member churches of CCT, notably the Roman Catholic, Lutheran, and Episcopal

Churches, have followed the tradition of relating
the first lesson closely to the gospel reading for
the day. The Common Lectionary (1983) had
largely departed from this practice, as already
noted, in the Sundays after Pentecost. The
Revised Common Lectionary has provided an
alternate set of first readings for the Sundays
after Pentecost, to meet the desire of these traditions that the eucharistic liturgy and its readings
be unified around the paschal mystery as it is
proclaimed in the gospel reading.[56]

The Evangelical Lutheran Church in America

The Evangelical Lutheran Church in America
reflects this concern in their decision to accept
only the gospel-related Old Testament lections in
Ordinary Time. The *RCL* lectionary tables are now
included in the denomination's worship calendars
and other worship resources. A complicating factor
in adopting the *RCL* is the church's long-standing
practice of celebrating lesser festivals on Sundays in
Ordinary Time and during Christmas. *The Lutheran
Book of Worship* allows lesser festivals to take
precedence on Sundays in Ordinary Time and on
the First and Second Sunday after Christmas.
During these periods worship leaders must be alert
to discrepancies between the two lectionary calendars. Disagreement exists within the church about
the treatment of Sunday. Some hold that Sundays

should always take precedence over lesser festivals. Each Sunday is to be seen as a feast of our Lord and should be held sacrosanct. Others feel that lesser festivals also hold out the pre-eminence of Jesus Christ and therefore celebrating the lesser festivals does not compromise the nature of Sundays.

The *RCL* has come down on the side of the centrality of Sunday:

> Lectionary tables and calendars are always inter-connected. At the heart of the particular way each calendar sets out its selected readings is a very basic view about our faith and our Christian way of life. The *Revised Common Lectionary* has taken the present Western calendar for Sundays, has simplified it to a certain extent by moving away from some recurring annual festivals with their distinctive themes, and has returned to a pattern of continuous or semi-continuous reading in one system for successive Lord's Days after Pentecost. The *Revised Common Lectionary* calendar contains both festival Sundays around the celebrations of Easter and Christmas, and the ordinary Sundays following the feasts of Epiphany and Pentecost.[57]

The Evangelical Lutheran Church in Canada

Despite the concern of some Lutherans regarding thematically related Old Testament texts, the Evangelical Lutheran Church in Canada chose to go with the semi-continuous track. This decision was made after extensive field testing of the lectionary, and because of the growing feeling that the Old Testament needs to be heard in its own context. Part of the positive response to the sequential reading came from people who liked the idea of 'restoring the old stories' they remembered. The *RCL* has been widely received across the church. The second reading is often dropped in the face of the more extensive first readings from the Old Testament. The lectionary is printed in a variety of worship resources published by the ELCIC.

The United Church of Canada

The United Church of Canada's new hymn book, *Voices United*, includes the entire *Revised Common Lectionary* tables making it readily accessible to worship planners and the congregation at large. The semi-continuous lections are shown in the tables for Ordinary Time along with the other appointed lections. A separate table lists the thematic track with the following notation: 'The following Old Testament and Psalm sets (thematically related to the Gospel) may be substituted for corresponding selections in the preceding list.' A high percentage of United Church congregations use the *Revised Common Lectionary*, though many omit the second reading.

The Revised Common Lectionary

The Christian Church (Disciples of Christ)

The Christian Church (Disciples of Christ) has accepted the *RCL* for optional use. Though the hymnal does not contain the *RCL* tables, the lectionary is readily available in a variety of worship resources published by the Christian Board of Publication. Only the sequential readings are listed for the Sundays after Pentecost. There is a growing use of the *RCL* within the denomination stimulated by the increasing use of *The Whole People of God* as the primary curriculum of congregations. A weekly bulletin series based on the *RCL* is published by the church as a further motivation to use the lectionary.

The Episcopal Church

The Episcopal Church in the United States is presently using the *RCL* in trial use for study and evaluation. This evaluative use of the lectionary was begun in 1994 following the 71st General Convention, and was re-authorized for continued evaluative use at the 1997 General Convention for the next triennium. Though only a limited number of congregations participated in the trial use during the first triennium, interest is growing as the *RCL* becomes more established ecumenically and within the provinces of the Anglican communion. Both tracks are authorized for the Sundays after Pentecost.

On Common Ground

The Anglican Church of Canada

The 1995 General Synod of the Anglican Church of Canada approved the *RCL* for use where authorized by the diocesan bishop. Only the semi-continuous track is authorized. The *RCL* has been met with wide acceptance across the church. The church made two minor alterations to the *RCL*. Because Psalm 51 is used in conjunction with a Litany of Penitence on Ash Wednesday, Psalm 103:8–18 (rather than Psalm 51, as appointed in *RCL*) is read at the Liturgy of the Word. A tenth reading at the Easter Vigil (Isaiah 54:5–14) included in *The Book of Alternative Services* remains an option for Anglicans not found in *RCL*. Readings are also proposed for festival and other days not covered by the *RCL*. Bulletin inserts and other resources are based on the *RCL*.

The Church of the Province of Southern Africa

When the Church of the Province of Southern Africa (Anglican) published *An Anglican Prayer Book 1989*, they included the original Common Lectionary as the authorized lectionary. For this reason, the church has not chosen to move for the adoption of the *RCL*. However, the thematically-related Old Testament lections from the *RCL* have been authorized for alternative use during Ordinary Time, and a

set of Old Testament readings for use during the
Easter season has also been added.

The Church of England

It is the Church of England that has made the most
dramatic changes in the *RCL* as it has adapted the
lectionary for use. It is important to note that the
1662 Book of Common Prayer is still the ultimate
authority for the ordering of worship in the Church
of England. *The Alternative Service Book 1980*
provides the liturgical texts and calendar that have
guided the life of the church in the late twentieth
century. The ASB included a two-year lectionary
based on a thematic approach to preaching and
interpretation. Over the years, there was a growing
consensus that this two-year lectionary was wearing
thin. *The Christian Year: Calendar, Lectionary and
Collects (CLC)*, incorporating the *RCL*, was authorized for use in the Church of England from the First
Sunday of Advent, 1997. It will remain an authorized option to the ASB lectionary until the year 2000
when *The Alternative Service Book 1980* will probably be withdrawn in favour of *CLC* and other new
service books, to be published under the generic
title, *Common Worship*.

The adaptations to the *RCL* taken by the Church
of England are outlined in some detail so that we
may understand the issues that lie behind the
changes made in the lectionary.[58]

First, the Revision Committee was concerned about what they considered omissions in the *RCL*. The theologically significant creation accounts from Genesis 1 and 2 are not appointed for Sunday reading in *RCL*. Genesis 1 is appointed by *RCL* as the first reading at the Easter Vigil, but the second creation account from Genesis 2 is not appointed at all. The Revision Committee also felt that the Book of Revelation deserved more attention than it receives in the ecumenical lectionary. To increase exposure to Genesis chapters 1 and 2, the Revision Committee introduced an emphasis on creation on the Second Sunday Before Lent in all three years (Year A – Genesis 1:1—2:3; Year B – 2:4b–9, 15–25; Year C – Proverbs 8:1, 22–31 – 'The Lord created me at the beginning of his work, the first of his works long ago.') This emphasis reflects the 9th Sunday before Christmas in the ASB lectionary when the theme was designated as 'creation Sunday'. This focus is also recognized in the 1662 Book of Common Prayer lectionary. Septuagesima Sunday and Sexagesima Sunday (3rd and 2nd Sundays before Lent) carry the theme of seed time and planting from the Gospel lections on these two Sundays (Matthew 20:1–16, the parable of the labourers in the vineyard, and Luke 8:4–15, the parable of the sower).

The addition of three lections from Revelation during Epiphany give further emphasis to this book in the version of the lectionary authorized by the Church of England. The additions come in Year B on the 2nd, 3rd, and 4th Sundays of Epiphany.

Notice a slightly different naming of the Sundays in what I have outlined so far. We have the Feast of the Epiphany in the adapted *RCL* followed by The Baptism of Christ, the First Sunday *of* Epiphany and then a Second, Third and Fourth Sunday *of* Epiphany, rather than Sundays *after* Epiphany. Next come three Sundays of Ordinary Time used as open Sundays when Easter falls late in the calendar. Finally, we have the Second Sunday Before Lent with its focus on creation followed by the Sunday Next Before Lent with the Transfiguration lections.

The Sundays of November provide another departure from the *RCL*. All Saints' Day ushers in a November emphasis on the kingship of Christ.

In the period from All Saints' Day to Advent Sunday, Sundays are designated 'before Advent', and bring together a cluster of themes that November provides – All Saints', the Departed, Remembrance and the Kingship of Christ. This brings the Christian year to an end with a celebration both of the reality of God's rule and the final ingathering into his kingdom... In the cycle of the seasons such an emphasis at the end of the year leads very naturally into the beginning of the new year, the season of Advent, when the same theme is developed from a slightly different angle. There is a long history of pre-Advent material that begins to anticipate what is to come, not least in the BCP provision for the Last Sunday after Trinity.[59]

These themes are already highlighted in the *RCL*, but are further emphasized in *CLC* with the designation of the Sundays Before Advent. Two gospel lections were changed over the three years of this pre-Advent season.

Note another major departure in *CLC*. Instead of Sundays after Pentecost, we find the Sundays after Trinity. This is in line with the long established designation of the Book of Common Prayer:

... Sundays through the summer have been named 'after Trinity', but the period of time to which it refers begins, not after Trinity Sunday itself, but a week earlier on the Monday after the Day of Pentecost. For that day marks a return to the non-seasonal Ordinary Time... Before Lent there is a comparatively short period of Ordinary Time. Now comes the much longer period stretching through to the end of the liturgical year.[60]

The Church of England's liturgical tradition calls for some additions to the calendar as presented by the *RCL*. The Day of Thanksgiving for Holy Communion (Corpus Christi) is one of those celebrations. *CLC* provides a full set of Propers for the

celebration of this festival on the Thursday following Trinity Sunday, including lections for Evening
Prayer before the feast day.

With Ordinary Time being shortened by the
November emphasis on the Reign of God, further
calendar changes happen in *CLC*. The Last Sunday
after Trinity comes the week before All Saints' Day.
The Collect appointed for that Sunday is Thomas
Cranmer's beloved prayer on the centrality of Scripture in the life of the faithful, 'Blessed Lord, who
caused all holy Scriptures to be written for our
learning ...'. With that Collect in mind, a full set
of lections for the three years are appointed for
optional use in congregations marking the Last
Sunday after Trinity as Bible Sunday. This theme
was traditionally attached to Advent 2 in the 1662
Book of Common Prayer, because that is the Sunday
Cranmer's Collect was appointed.[61] Another tradition of special significance to the Church of England
is the Dedication Festival which can be celebrated
on the first Sunday in October or on this last Sunday
after Trinity. The occasion remembers the dedication of the local parish church and can be transferred
to another Sunday that is significant to that parish.

Speaking of Collects, *CLC* provides dated lections
with Proper numbers as in *RCL*. However, Collects
appointed for specific Sundays after Trinity are
printed in a separate section. Thus the same Collect
(and post-communion prayer) will always be heard
on the same Sunday after Trinity, but the lections

will be determined by the *calendar* date (e.g. Proper 25 – the Sunday between 23 and 29 October inclusive).

Other calendar changes affect the way the *RCL* is adapted by the Church of England. After the four Sundays of Advent comes a distinct *season* of Christmas. Traditionally, we tend to think of the season of the twelve days of Christmas, but the *RCL* follows the practice of naming the two Sundays *after* Christmas. *CLC*, on the other hand, clearly names the First and Second Sunday *of* Christmas with a note saying, 'The days after Christmas Day until the Epiphany traditionally form a unity of days of special thanksgiving.'[62]

The three major narratives associated with Epiphany are the visit of the Magi, the baptism of Jesus and the miracle at Cana. The *RCL*, following the *Roman Lectionary for Mass* 1969, appoints John 2:1–11 only in Year C on the Second Sunday after Epiphany. With *CLC*, congregations hear the Cana story in all three years. The lections appointed by *RCL* and included in *CLC* emphasize Jesus' first acts of power and witness as the Sundays after Epiphany unfold: 'And a report about him began to reach every place in the region' (Luke 4:37).

A brief period of Ordinary Time begins after The Presentation, but the Sundays are numbered '... next before Lent', with the Sunday before Lent carrying the Transfiguration narrative.

Lent presents two changes to the *RCL* lections.

Long tradition within the Church of England associates the Fourth Sunday of Lent with Mothering Sunday, echoing the traditional epistle lection from the Book of Common Prayer: 'Jerusalem ... which is the mother of us all' (Galatians 4:26). With this tradition in mind, an alternative set of lections is appointed for this Sunday using either Luke 2:33–35 (Simeon's words to Mary foreseeing that 'a sword will pierce your own soul too') or John 19:25–27 (Mary at the foot of the Cross) as the gospel.

The Fifth Sunday of Lent is given a subheading, 'Passiontide begins'. This has no effect, however, on the appointed lections but has more to do with setting the focus for what is to come. The lections for this Sunday continue the baptismal themes of Lent that prepare catechumens and the congregation for baptism at the Easter Vigil.

The Great Fifty Days of Easter follow the *RCL*, but with a nine-day period of preparation for Pentecost beginning with the Friday after Ascension. 'The nine days are a Pentecost sub-season within Eastertide, rather as Passiontide is a sub-season within Lent.'[63]

Alternative psalmody is offered '... to reduce the numbers of verses of a particular provision and, in others, to simplify the reading'.[64] (*RCL* for Easter 3, Year A, has Psalm 116:1–4, 12–19; *CLC*, for the same Sunday, has Psalm 116:1–8).

Two other departures from the *RCL* are significant to note. First, during Ordinary Time, congrega-

tions may depart from the formal lectionary: '...
after due consultation with the Parochial Church
Council, the minister may, from time to time,
depart from the lectionary for pastoral reasons or
preaching or teaching purposes'. Secondly, three sets
of lections are provided for every Sunday of the
three-year cycle. 'The Principal Service Lectionary
(which is drawn from the *Revised Common Lectionary*) is intended for use at the principal service of
the day (whether this service is Holy Communion
or some other authorized form).'[66] The Second
Service Lectionary may be used when the congregation has more than one service on a Sunday. Finally,
a Third Service Lectionary is provided, with shorter
readings appropriate for the Daily Office:

> ... the Church of England has produced comple-
> mentary lectionaries for second and third services
> on a Sunday. They use passages not in the *Revised
> Common Lectionary*, or not in it in that particular
> year. Like it, they are seasonal yet not thematic,
> and employ a semi-continuous approach to books
> especially in 'ordinary time'. Few readings in the
> ASB revision fail to find a place in one of the three
> lectionaries, and many passages, which did not
> feature in ASB, have found their way back in.[67]

The Anglican Church in Australia

A Prayer Book for Australia: Liturgical Resources

Authorised by the General Synod, 1995 (The Anglican Church of Australia) is to be used in conjunction with the 1662 Book of Common Prayer and *An Australian Prayer Book* (1978). The new publication includes the *RCL* with both tracks authorized for Ordinary Time. In addition, the book follows the Church of England pattern by offering a second set of readings for each Sunday. 'The second set of readings supplements the first (*RCL*) set. It assumes that those present either have been or will be present at the service where the first set of readings are used. Since the same congregation would not normally celebrate the Holy Communion twice on the same day, the second set includes one reading from each testament.'[68] There are some lections taken from the Church of England's second or third services, but on the whole this series seems to be unique to the book.

Conclusions

Some thirty-five churches across the world are now using the *Common Lectionary* or the *RCL*. Other churches are considering adopting the *RCL* while still others use some form of the three year lectionary based on the *Roman Lectionary for Mass,* 1969. Thus the *RCL* has become a major ecumenical document! Christians gather to praise God each Sunday and their common praise is shaped by a common lectionary. The effects of this ecumenical consensus are bound to draw us a step closer to Jesus' prayer that we may all be one.

> I ask not only on behalf of these, but also on behalf of those who will believe in me through their word, that they may all be one. As you, Father, are in me and I am in you, may they also be in us, so that the world may believe that you have sent me. The glory that you have given me I have given them, so that they may be one as we are one. I in them and you in me, that they become completely one, so that the world may know that you have sent me and have loved them even as you have loved me. (John 17:20–23)

Acknowledgements

The following people were most helpful in gathering the data presented above:

- American Baptist Churches – the Revd Larry W. Dobson
- Anglican Church of Canada – the Revd Paul Gibson, Toronto, Ontario
- Christian Church (Disciples of Christ) – Dr Sally Smith, St. Louis, Missouri
- Christian Reformed Church in North America – Dr Emily Brink, Grand Rapids, Michigan

The Revised Common Lectionary

- Church of England – the Revd Dr Donald Gray, Westminster Abbey, London
- Church of the Province of Southern Africa (Anglican) – the Revd Cynthia Botha, Marshalltown, Johannesburg
- Evangelical Lutheran Church in America – the Revd Paul Nelson and the Revd Karen Ward, Chicago, Illinois
- Evangelical Lutheran Church in Canada – the Revd André Lavergne, New Hamburg, Ontario
- Presbyterian Church in Canada – the Revd Dianne J. Strickland, Winnipeg, Manitoba
- Presbyterian Church, USA – the Revd Horace T. Allen, Jr
- Scottish Episcopal Church – Gianfranco Tellini, Dunblane
- United Church of Canada – Dr Fred Graham, Etobicoke, Ontario
- United Church of Christ – Mr Arthur Clyde, Cleveland, Ohio
- United Methodist Church – the Revd Hoyt L. Hickman, Nashville, Tennessee

PART THREE

CHAPTER 6

Titles of Sundays and Special Days

The following is a list of the Sundays and Special Days included in the *Revised Common Lectionary*. Each Church may then choose how to name each set of Sundays and Special Days, and whether or not to include all of these days in its own lectionary.

Season of Advent

First Sunday of Advent	Sunday between November 27 and December 3
Second Sunday of Advent	Sunday between December 4 and December 10
Third Sunday of Advent	Sunday between December 11 and December 17
Fourth Sunday of Advent	Sunday between December 18 and December 24

Season of Christmas

Nativity of the Lord (Christmas Day)	December 25

First Sunday after Christmas	Sunday between December 26 and January 1
New Year's Day	January 1
Second Sunday after Christmas	Sunday between January 2 and January 5

*Season of Epiphany (Ordinary Time)**

Epiphany of the Lord	January 6 or First Sunday in January
First Sunday after the Epiphany [1] (Baptism of the Lord)	Sunday between January 7 and January 13
Second Sunday after the Epiphany [2]	Sunday between January 14 and January 20
Third Sunday after the Epiphany [3]	Sunday between January 21 and January 27
Fourth Sunday after the Epiphany [4]	Sunday between January 28 and February 3
Fifth Sunday after the Epiphany [5]	Sunday between February 4 and February 10
Sixth Sunday after the Epiphany [6] (Proper 1, except when this Sunday is the Last Sunday after the Epiphany)	Sunday between February 11 and February 17
Seventh Sunday after the Epiphany [7] (Proper 2, except when this Sunday is the Last Sunday after the Epiphany)	Sunday between February 18 and February 24
Eighth Sunday after the Epiphany [8] (Proper 3, except when this Sunday is the Last Sunday after the Epiphany)	Sunday between February 25 and February 29

Titles of Sundays and Special Days

Ninth Sunday after the Epiphany [9] (Proper 4, for Churches that do not observe the Last Sunday after the Epiphany with Transfiguration readings)

Sunday between March 1 and March 7

Last Sunday after the Epiphany (Transfiguration Sunday)

Season of Lent

Ash Wednesday

First Sunday in Lent

Second Sunday in Lent

Third Sunday in Lent

Fourth Sunday in Lent

Fifth Sunday in Lent

Sixth Sunday in Lent
(Passion Sunday or Palm Sunday)

Holy Week
  Monday of Holy Week
  Tuesday of Holy Week
  Wednesday of Holy Week
  Holy Thursday
  Good Friday
  Holy Saturday

Season of Easter

Resurrection of the Lord
  Easter Vigil

On Common Ground

Easter Day

Second Sunday of Easter

Third Sunday of Easter

Fourth Sunday of Easter

Fifth Sunday of Easter

Sixth Sunday of Easter

Ascension of the Lord
(Fortieth day, Sixth Thursday of Easter)

Seventh Sunday of Easter

Day of Pentecost

Season after Pentecost (Ordinary Time)*

Trinity Sunday
(First Sunday after Pentecost)

Propers 4–28 (9–33)
(Second to Twenty-Sixth
Sunday after Pentecost)

Proper 29 (34)   Sunday between November
(Reign of Christ or Christ   20 and November 26
the King, Last Sunday after
Pentecost)

Special Days

February 2 – Presentation of the Lord

March 25 – Annunciation of the Lord

May 31 – Visitation of Mary to Elizabeth

September 14 – Holy Cross

Titles of Sundays and Special Days

November 1 – All Saints

Fourth Thursday of November (U.S.), Second Monday of
  October (Can.) – Thanksgiving Day

* Note: Since Easter is a movable feast, it can occur as
early as March 22 and as late as April 25. When Easter is
early, it encroaches on the Sundays after the Epiphany,
reducing their number, as necessary, from as many as
nine to as few as four. In similar fashion, the date of
Easter determines the number of Sunday Propers after
Pentecost. When Easter is as early as March 22, the
numbered Proper for the Sunday following Trinity Sunday is Proper 3.

The Propers in [brackets] indicate the Proper number-
ing system of the Roman Catholic Church and the
Anglican Church of Canada.

CHAPTER 7

Members of the *Revised Common Lectionary* Task Force

The task force that prepared the *Revised Common Lectionary* was appointed by the Consultation on Common Texts in November of 1986. The membership has involved persons whose Churches and liturgical conferences actively use the *Common Lectionary*, have tested the *Common Lectionary*, or have a serious interest in adopting the *Revised Common Lectionary* for use. The members of the task force included:

The Reverend Dr Neil Alexander, Professor of Worship at General Seminary in New York City, representative of the Lutheran Churches from 1986–1987.

The Reverend Dr Horace T. Allen, Jr, Professor of Worship and Preaching at Boston University School of Theology, representative of the English Language Liturgical Consultation, member of the committee that created

Members of the RCL Task Force

the 1983 Common Lectionary, and representative of the Presbyterian Church (USA).

The Reverend Robert J. Brooks, The Presiding Bishop's Staff Officer of the Episcopal Church: Washington Office, member of the Standing Liturgical Commission (1985–1988), and representative of the Episcopal Church.

The Reverend Dr Thomas D. Dipko, Bishop of the Ohio Area of the United Church of Christ, and representative of the United Church of Christ.

The Reverend John Fitzsimmons, Chairperson of the Advisory Committe of the International Commission on English in the Liturgy (ICEL), Roman Catholic, and representative of the English Language Liturgical Consultation (ELLC), beginning in 1990.

The Reverend Paul Gibson, Liturgical Officer of the Anglican Church of Canada, Chair of the Consultation on Common Texts from 1986–1989, and representative of the Anglican Church of Canada.

Dr Fred Graham, Consultant on Congregational Worship and representative of the United Church of Canada, beginning in 1988.

The Reverend Canon Dr Donald Gray, Canon of Westminster, Church of England, Chairman of the Joint Liturgical Group (JLG) of Great Britain, and representative of the English Language Liturgical Consultation (ELLC).

On Common Ground

The Reverend Dr Gerald Hobbs, Professor of Church History, Vancouver School of Theology, Vancouver, British Columbia, the United Church of Canada, Standing Consultant with particular focus on the psalms, beginning in 1989.

The Reverend Canon Dr David R. Holeton, Professor in Divinity at Trinity College, Toronto, and representative of the Anglican Church of Canada.

The Reverend Thomas A. Langford, III, Assistant General Secretary of The Section on Worship of The United Methodist Church, Chair of the Task Force on the *Revised Common Lectionary*, and representative of the United Methodist Church.

The Reverend Edward Matthews, past Secretary of Liturgical Office of the Bishops' Conference of England and Wales, Roman Catholic, member of the Joint Liturgical Group (JLG) of Great Britain, member of the Advisory Committe of the International Commission on English in the Liturgy (ICEL), and representative of the English Language Liturgical Consultation (ELLC), 1988–1989.

The Reverend Dr Fred McNally, Consultant on Congregational Worship and representative of the United Church of Canada, 1988–1989.

Dr Gail Ramshaw, Professor of Religion at LaSalle University, and representative of the Evangelical Lutheran Church in America, 1987–1992.

Notes

Introduction

1. Vatican II, *Dogmatic Constitution on Divine Revelation, Dei verbum*, 18 November 1965.
2. Horace T. Allen, Jr, 'The Liturgical Use of Scripture', *Reformed Liturgy and Music*, Vol. XXIV, No. 4, Fall 1990, p. 167.
3. Karl Barth, *Church Dogmatics, Vol. I, Part I* (trans. G. T. Thompson; Edinburgh, T. & T. Clark, 1936), pp. 89–90.
4. Karl Barth, *The Word of God and the Word of Man* (trans. Douglas Horton; London, Hodder and Stoughton, 1928), p. 106.

Chapter 1

5. Vatican II, *The Constitution on the Sacred Liturgy, Sacrosanctum concilium*, 4 December 1963, para. 51.
6. Gaston Fontaine, CRIC, *Commentarium ad Ordinem Lectionum Missae, Notitiae*, no. 47 (1969, 258, unpublished, trans. International Commission on English in the Liturgy).

7. Kathleen Hughes, RSCJ, *The Monk's Tale* (Collegeville, MA, The Liturgical Press, 1991), p. 252.
8. Sacred Congregation for Divine Worship, *Ordo lectionum Missae*: (Rome: Vatican Polyglot Press, 25 May 1969).
9. Sacred Congregation for the Sacraments and Divine Worship, *Lectionary for Mass*, Second *Editio Typica*, 1981.
10. *Common Lectionary: The Lectionary Proposed by the Consultation on Common Texts* (New York, The Church Hymnal Corporation, 1983), p. 8.
11. *New Catholic Encyclopedia*, XVII 'Consultation on Common Texts' by Horace T. Allen, Jr.
12. Minutes of the Consultation on Common Texts (Washington, DC) 28–31 March 1978.
13. Horace T. Allen, Jr, 'Address to *Societas Liturgica*', mimeographed (Paris, 25 August 1981).
14. Consultation on Common Texts, *The Revised Common Lectionary* (Norwich, The Canterbury Press, 1992).
15. International Consultation on English Texts, *Prayers We Have in Common* (Philadelphia, Fortress Press, 1970, 1971 and 1975).
16. Minutes of The English Language Liturgical Consultation, August 1985 (Boston, MA).
17. Minutes of The English Language Liturgical Consultation, August 1987 (Brixen, Italy).
18. Frederick R. McManus, 'Pastoral Ecumenism', in Martin Connell (ed.), *Eucharist – Toward the Third Millennium* (Chicago, Liturgy Training Publications, 1997), p. 116.

Notes

Chapter 2

19. James F. White, *Documents of Christian Worship* (Louisville, KY, Westminster/John Knox Press, 1992), p. 101.
20. White, *Documents of Christian Worship*, p. 109.
21. White, *Documents of Christian Worship*, p. 101.
22. Karl-Heinrich Bieritz, 'The Order of Readings and Sermon Texts for the German Lutheran Church', *Studia Liturgica* 21 (1991), p. 37.
23. *Sacrosanctum concilium*, para. 52.
24. trans. John Wilkerson, *Egeria's Travels to the Holy Land* (Warminster, England, Aris & Phillips 1981), p. 26.
25. Thomas J. Talley, *The Origins of the Liturgical Year* (New York, Pueblo, 1986).
26. John Gunstone, 'Contemporary Problems of Liturgical Time: Calendar and Lectionary', *Studia Liturgica* 14 (1982), pp. 74–5.
27. Gunstone, 'Contemporary Problems of Liturgical Time', pp. 74–5.
28. *Lectionary for Mass*, Second *Editio Typica*, para. 30.
29. Consultation on Common Texts (1983), pp. 21–22.
30. Horace T. Allen, Jr, 'Preaching and Lectionary', in Martin Dudley (ed.), *Like a Two-edged Sword: Essays in Honour of Canon Donald Gray* (Norwich, The Canterbury Press, 1995).
31. Raymond E. Brown, *The Churches the Apostles Left Behind* (New York, Paulist Press, 1984).
32. James A. Sanders, *Torah and Canon* (Philadelphia, Westminster Press, 1972).

33. James A. Sanders, *Canon and Community* (Philadelphia, Westminster Press, 1984).
34. James A. Sanders, *God Has A Story Too: Sermons in Context* (Philadelphia, Westminster Press, 1979).
35. Barth, *The Word of God*, p. 33.
36. Barth, *The Word of God*, p. 34.

Chapter 3

37. Fritz West, *Scripture and Memory: The Ecumenical Hermeneutic of the Three-Year Lectionaries* (Collegeville, MN, The Liturgical Press, 1997).
38. West, *Scripture and Memory*, p. xi.
39. West, *Scripture and Memory*, p. xi.
40. West, *Scripture and Memory*, p. 5.
41. West, *Scripture and Memory*, p. 5.
42. Dieter T. Hessel (ed.), *Social Themes of the Christian Year: A Commentary on the Lectionary* (Philadelphia, Geneva Press, 1983).
43. Hessel (ed.), *Social Themes of the Christian Year*, p. 258.
44. Hessel (ed.), *Social Themes of the Christian Year*, p. 258.
45. Hessel (ed.), *Social Themes of the Christian Year*, p. 262.
46. West, *Scripture and Memory*, p. 15.
47. West, *Scripture and Memory*, p. 12.
48. West's admittedly speculative but also very suggestive footnote on this development (n. 24 in Ch. 1) is well worth careful reflection, certainly for North American readers.
49. West, *Scripture and Memory*, pp. 18–19.

Notes

Chapter 4

50. Pontifical Biblical Commission, 'Document on the Interpretation of the Bible in the Church' (23 April, 1993), IV, c., 1.
51. Horace T. Allen, Jr, 'Address to the Congregation of Divine Worship and the Discipline of the Sacraments' (19 May 1994), mimeographed document, 4.
52. *The Tablet* (7 November 1997).
53. *St Vladimir's Theological Quarterly*, Vol. 41. 2–3 (1997), p. 137.
54. *St Vladimir's Theological Quarterly*, Vol. 41. 2–3 (1997), pp. 137–38.

Chapter 5

55. *Leaders Guide for Adults, Year 3, The Inviting Word: A Worship-centered, Lectionary-based Curriculum for Congregations* (Cleveland OH, United Church Press, 1996).
56. *Revised Common Lectionary* (Nashville, TN, Abingdon Press, 1992) p. 18.
57. *Revised Common Lectionary*, p. 13.
58. I am especially grateful to the Revd Dr Donald Gray, Westminster Abbey, for helping me to understand the important issues that shaped the adaptation of the *RCL* by the Church of England.
59. *The Christian Year: Calendar, Lectionary and Collects* (London, Church House Publishing 1997) pp. 242–43.
60. Michael Perham, *Celebrate the Christian Story: An*

Introduction to the New Lectionary and Calendar (London, SPCK, 1997) p. 79.
61. Perham, *Celebrate the Christian Story*, p. 83.
62. *The Christian Year*, p. 17.
63. Perham, *Celebrate the Christian Story*, p. 78.
64. *The Christian Year*, p. 95.
65. *The Christian Year*, p. 36. See also pp. 248–49.
66. *The Christian Story*, p. 37.
67. Perham, *Celebrate the Christian Story*, p. 27.
68. *A Prayer Book For Australia* (Broughton Books, 1995) p. 462.